THE AZTECS' MANY GODS

HISTORY BOOKS BEST SELLERS

Children's History Books

Speedy Publishing LLC
40 E. Main St. #1156
Newark, DE 19711
www.speedypublishing.com
Copyright 2017

All Rights reserved. No part of this book may be reproduced or used in any way or form or by any means whether electronic or mechanical, this means that you cannot record or photocopy any material ideas or tips that are provided in this book.

The Aztec Empire was a great culture in what is now Mexico and Central America. Who were their gods and what were they like? Let's find out!

A Culture of Gods

The Aztec Empire was at its strongest between 1350 and 1520 CE. It was a culture with many gods, and the Aztecs, like the ancient Greeks and Romans, thought the gods had a hand in everything. There were gods for the weather, for war, and for the harvest. A lot of Aztec cultural activity involved ceremonies or sacrifices to please the gods.

Aztec god

You can compare these gods to those of the Greeks by reading the Baby Professor book The Greek Gods and Heroes. And the Baby Professor book The World is Full of Spirits can tell you about what the Aztecs' northern neighbors believed in what is now the United States.

THE CHIEF GODS

The Aztecs had over 200 gods and goddesses. They were in three groups:

- Gods of the sky
- Gods of the rain and growing things
- Gods of sacrifice and war

**Tlaloc
God of the Rain and Growing things**

HUITZILOPOCHTLI

HERE ARE SOME OF THE MAIN GODS

HUITZILOPOCHTLI

Huitzilopochtli was the primary god of the Aztecs. In their myths, he told the Aztecs how to leave their home in Aztalan and where to make their new city. That city, Tenochtitlan, is now Mexico City.

Although Huitzilopochtli means "hummingbird on the left", he was a war god. His temple was covered with images of skulls and painted blood-red.

The Aztecs believed Huitzilopochtli appeared in the sky as an eagle, and they founded Tenochtitlan where priests saw an eagle standing on a rock, eating a snake.

Huitzilopochtli was not just a war god for the fun of it. He led the fight of good against evil. He required blood, and sometimes human sacrifice, so he could fight off evil spirits and dark forces and keep humans safe. People honored him for this effort, and built temples where they could worship him in the center of Aztec cities. There was a picture of Huitzilopochtli on the throne of Moctezuma, the last great leader of the Aztecs.

TLALOC

Tlaloc was the god of rain, and one of the oldest gods in the region. Before the Aztecs, the Olmec and Mayans worshiped Tlaloc. His temple in Tenochtitlan had blue decorations that looked like rain and water. Tlaloc could send rainstorms, hail, and thunder when he was mad at the people.

    The Aztecs believed that Tlaloc loved the tears of babies.

CHALCHIUHTLICUE

She was the patron of rivers, streams, and all that lived in them, and of childbirth. In pictures, she has a blue-green skirt out of which a river is flowing. It makes sense that in Aztec myths she is in love with Tlaloc, since they both have so much to do with water.

CHALCHIUHTLICUE

The face of Tonatiuh, from the central disk of an Aztec calendar

TONATIUH

Tonatiuh was the god of the sun. He brought warmth to both people and crops. But to do this, he needed sacrifices of blood. Sometimes, just a cup of blood would do; but most of the time his worship involved human sacrifice. He was also the patron god of Aztec fighters.

CAMAXTLI

This was the god of war, like the Greek god Ares and the Roman god Mars. He also was the creator of fire, the patron of hunters, and the god of fate (what is going to happen to a person). The Aztecs believed that Camaxtli, with three other gods, created the whole world.

TEZCATLIPOCA

This god's name means "mirror of smoke", and he is the god of the night, of the north, and of evil things. He is sort of the opposite of his brother, the feathered serpent Quetzalcoatl. In pictures of him, he has a black mirror and wears dark stripes across his face.

QUETZALCÓATL

Tezcatlipoca's brother, Quetzalcóatl, is worshiped in many cultures in Central America and what is now Mexico. He was the god of learning, wisdom, knowledge, and creativity. He would be a lot more fun to be around than his brother would be!

OTHER INTERESTING GODS

Some of the lesser gods also played important parts in Aztec culture and spiritual life:

CENTEOTL

He was the god of corn, an essential part of the Native American diet. Many cultures worshiped him under various names. In pictures, he is a young man with a corn cob growing from his crown.

XIPE TOTEC

This god's name means "the god with his skin peeled off", which sounds horrible! But the meaning is that he is responsible for new growth and fertility, for casting off the old and putting on the new. He sheds his skin the way a snake sheds its skin, in order to grow a fresh, new one.

Xipe Totec

Mayahuel

MAYAHUEL

She was the goddess of the maguey plant, or aloe, which gave sweet sap that was important to Aztec cooking. Her other name is "the woman with four hundred breasts" who can feed all the Aztecs, her children.

TLALTECHUTLI

This terrible goddess controlled the horizon of the Earth, and every day swallowed up the sun so night could cover the sky. She required many blood sacrifices to make her let the sun come back.

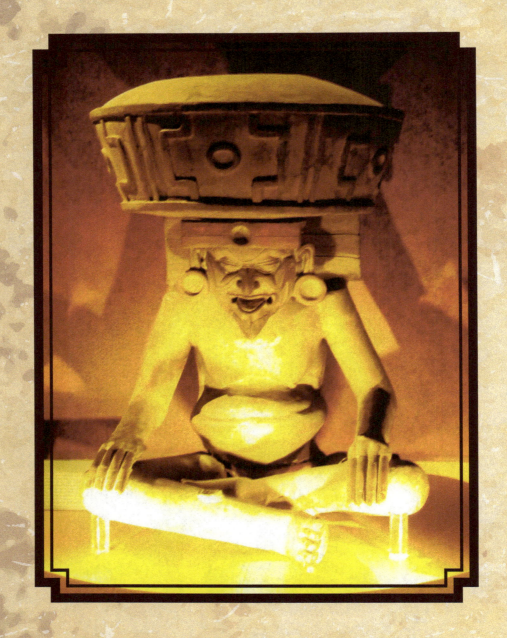

HUEHUETEOTL

HUEHUETEOTL

Huehueteotl was considered the very oldest god, and was the patron of fire. Every Aztec home had a little altar where the family worshiped Huehueteotl. The household worship was much milder than the sacrifices to the god in public ceremonies! His elements were fire and blood, and he demanded a lot of both.

OMETEOTL

This god is actually two gods, and the Aztecs thought of them as the parents of the major gods. They were not really husband and wife, but more like two sides of the creative force of the universe. The male half was Ometecuhtli and the female half was Omecihuatl. In pictures, this god often appears as a half-male, half-female figure.

Ometeotl

DIVINE FACTS ABOUT THE AZTEC GODS

Here are some other things to know about the gods of the Aztecs:

- Most of the gods had two faces, meaning that they had both a positive and a negative side.
- Only one third of the gods were female.

The need to make lots of human sacrifices guided Aztec political life. They spent a lot of energy in wars against their neighbors, so they could capture fighters of other cultures and use them for sacrifice. However, faithful Aztecs often willingly offered themselves for sacrifice, even very painful things that we would think of as torture, to honor their gods. The sacrifices were often the central events of huge rituals at the temples in the middle of their capital, Tenochtitlan.

The worship of the god Tezcatlipoca involved a handsome young man, usually a prisoner of war. The prisoner lived like a prince for a month, enjoying every pleasure as if he were a god. Then, on the day of sacrifice his heart was torn out on the flat top of a small temple.

Ometecuhtli was one of the great gods of life, but the Aztecs never built him a temple. Although they kept him in mind in every ritual, they felt he was too far away in the heavens to even notice if they worshiped him.

Huitzilopochtli was born after his mother, Coatlicue, found a bunch of hummingbird feathers and put them inside her blouse.

Xochiquetal   Xochipilli

Xochiquetal and Xochipilli were twins. Xochiquetal, the sister, controlled aspects of art, growing plants, and love. She was captured and taken to the underworld after she ate some forbidden fruit, like Demeter in Greek mythology. Xochipilli, her brother, was like the Greek god Dionysus, the patron of games, songs, dance, and celebration.

The Aztecs believed that Quetzalcóatl created people. But the story is more complicated than that! By the time Quetzalcóatl got around to making humans, they had already been created—three times! Each time they destroyed each other by fighting. Quetzalcóatl went into the underworld, collected human bones from the past creations, and added his own blood to them to make a new generation of humans.

For the Aztecs, the spirits of all women who died in childbirth continued to live within the goddess Cihuateteo. Aztecs considered childbirth a dangerous battle with the world, equal to fighting in a war, and honored women who died while having babies the same way they honored great fighters.

Cihuateteco also had a wilder side, though. She and the spirits of women were supposed to haunt places where two roads crossed, and to confuse the minds of people who passed such a crossroad at night.

At its height, the Aztec Empire included over six million people, many of whom had been part of other cultures and civilizations. The Aztecs often absorbed the most interesting or most powerful gods from these cultures and added them to their own religious system.

Aztec gods were not immortal. They could die, and after they could be reborn. In some of the myths some of the gods willingly sacrifice themselves to start the world turning and to prevent disasters, but they are reborn soon after.

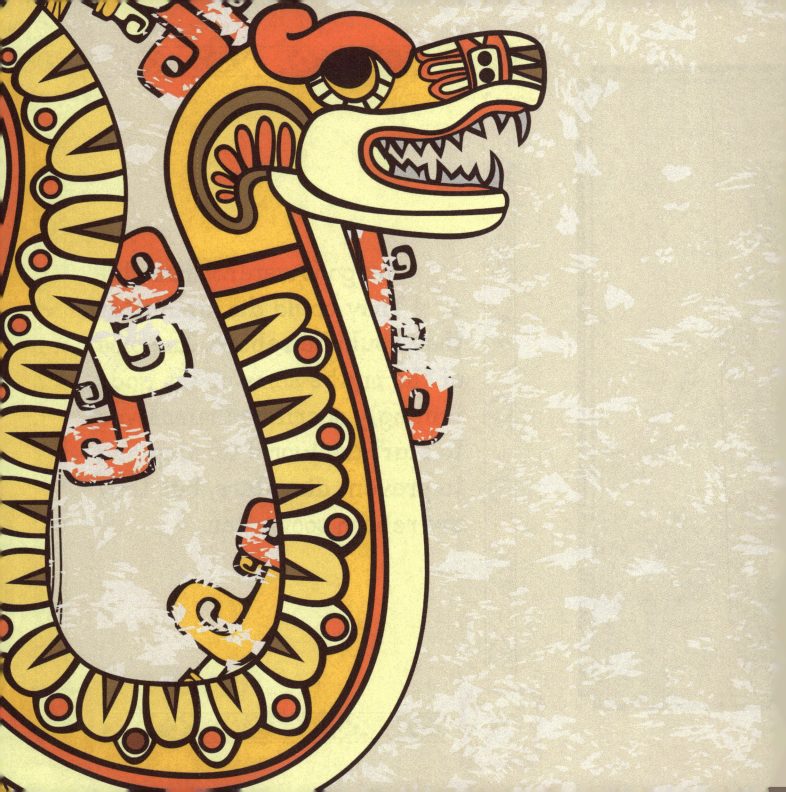

Learn More About the Aztecs

The Aztec civilization was complicated and interesting. Learn more about it, and what happened to it, in Baby Professor books like Aztec Technology and Art and The Spanish Conquistadors Conquer the Aztecs.

Visit

BABY PROFESSOR
EDUCATION KIDS

www.BabyProfessorBooks.com

to download Free Baby Professor eBooks
and view our catalog of new and exciting
Children's Books

Milton Keynes UK
Ingram Content Group UK Ltd.
UKHW050926310824
447642UK00002B/124

9 798869 410832